Chosen

ELISA DOMINGUEZ

Copyright © 2021 Elisa Dominguez
All rights reserved
First Edition

PAGE PUBLISHING, INC.
Conneaut Lake, PA

First originally published by Page Publishing 2021

ISBN 978-1-6624-5551-3 (pbk)
ISBN 978-1-6624-5552-0 (digital)

Printed in the United States of America

Praising God above all for his love and grace.

Thank you to my sister Brenda and her husband for being my cheerleaders and helping me through one of the toughest times in my life. To my brother Christian, I'm so proud to be your sister.

My boys Damien and Dariel, I hope to make you proud. I love you.

Special thanks to My friend and sister in Christ Maribel Juarez, the illustrator of this book for her beautiful artwork and dedication.

For more information, contact her at
cover art and illustrations done by
Maribel Juarez:
IG: mari.bellarte012
mmamcd4@yahoo.com

I want to be able to express my love for God and bring hope to others through my poetry and by writing this book. I hope to see that no matter what we may be going through in life, God is with us every step of the way. We are not alone.

It has been during this time where I have gone through several battles in my life that allowed me to get to know my true self. Growing up, I remember being a very timid and intuitive person. I felt like an outcast because of my personality. Thankfully, I was blessed by God at birth because I was born at the same time as my best friend. How amazing is that? My twin and I were born on August of 1986, and it is by the grace of God that we are alive.

Only God can do these miraculous things and for a great purpose—to show his mighty power within each of us. He does it in such a way, so tenderly, that it takes time to know why we go through certain battles in our lives. We go through life making mistakes that can drastically change the route of our lives, either by our decisions or by the way we were raised. I know that growing up we both felt the rejection and lack of validation and love from our mother. But God knew that we would need each other to be able to breeze through life, and make us stronger as we always had each other to lean on.

It was throughout the lengthy process of a divorce, God gave me the strength to leave this marriage. My husband was a very abusive man, both mentally and physically, and it was almost twelve years of an abusive relationship. I am still in the process of finalizing the divorce, and I had begun to journal my thoughts, my emotions, my prayers, and my conversations with God. I realized that I had the privilege to be able to express myself very well through my writing. I had shared my poetry with my sister and my fellow brothers and sisters in Christ. They are the only true family that I have, my family in Christ. They have been loving and supportive to me and my children. There is more to my story that I would like to share—from the rejection of our mother, our family, and how my sister and I had only each other.

I will be sharing a series of poems that I have written, inspired by God. A few of them are just inspired by love—a love that I hope to have one day. Behind every poem, there is a story waiting to be told.

Al escribir este libro quisiera poder expresar mi amor y gratitud hacia Dios, por medio de la poesía. Que aquel que lo lea pueda encontrar la esperanza que Jesús nos da. No importa las circunstancias que podremos estar pasando, Dios está con nosotros. No estamos solos. Dios va con nosotros cada paso que damos.

Ha sido durante esta etapa de mi vida que he pasado por varias batallas, En las que me he podido conocer a mi misma. Durante mi niñez y como fui creciendo. Siempre fui muy tímida, pero muy intuitiva. Dado que era muy tímida eso me hacía sentir diferente a otros.

Gracias a Dios, que al nacer fui bendecida con mi mejor amiga. Ya que somos gemelas. Que increíble es Dios que el sabia que necesitaría a una compañera de vida. Nacimos en el año 1986. Y fue por un milagro que estamos vivas. Solo Dios puede hacer esos milagros y maravillas y con un gran propósito. Para poder mostrar su enorme poder en cada una de nuestras vidas. En el transcurso de nuestra crianza (mi gemela y yo) sentimos el rechazo y falta de amor y maltrato de nuestra madre, en donde nuestra relación entre mi hermana y yo fue lo que nos mantuvo fuertes y siempre cuidando uno de la otra. Hay veces que nos cuesta entender porque pasamos por ciertas cosas. Pasamos por la vida cometiendo errores o hay veces que por lo que hemos pasado durante nuestra crianza que puede llevarnos a ciertos caminos difíciles. Pero no imposibles de sobre llevar. Dios muestra su poder de una manera muy tierna y poderosa que se puede ver.

Durante el proceso de la separación y divorcio, Dios me di o las fuerzas para poder dejar una relación llena de abuso y maltrato, no solo físico, pero también emocional. En el tiempo de este proceso largo, comencé a escribir mis pensamientos, emociones, he oraciones, y conversaciones con Dios. Y al escribir me di cuenta del privilegio que se me ha dado de poder expresarme de tal manera por medio de la escritura. He compartido mi poesía con mi hermana gemela, y con mis hermanas y hermanos en Cristo. Que son la única y verdadera familia que tengo. Mi familia espiritual. Ellos han sido de gran apoyo, para mis hijos y yo.

Estos poemas son inspirados por Dios, y otros son basados en el Amor. Un amor que anhelo algún día tener. Detrás de cada poema hay una historia.

The One

The paths I took,
Mistakes I made,
Caused me to feel enormous shame,
Because my world was full of pain.
I felt the need to numb myself
With worldly things, full of despair.
The day I wanted (it) to end,
You sent a person, a dear friend
To cross my path and speak the word,
The knowledge that would change my world!
Your plan for me, to know the truth,
Would be the light for me to chase,
The One who fills that empty space,
The One who is,
The One who saves.
You saved my life.
Your warm embrace,
The only One that I will praise!

CRAFTED BY LOVE

My timidness, being soo shy...
I always felt it was a flaw!
I would discover after time
It was a blessing in disguise!
I heard a whisper...

It was You!
A voice I knew I heard before
Impacted me in such a way.
It's so profound I can't explain...

Although I feel that I may lack,
My timidness isn't a setback,
Each detail of my temperament

Your perfect plan, for me to be
The girl that I was meant to be,
Your Spirit makes my thoughts become Alive!
Filled with Hope, full of life!

Beloved Rose

Like pieces of a broken vase,
My heart is shattered
With so much pain.
Your Word has told me
That I am free
No matter what.
You're all I need,
You spoke to me in a dream.
"Part of your story, you'll have to tell.
The hurt you feel,
The wounds you have
Are part of you, that I will heal."
Don't be ashamed,
Don't be afraid,
I'll tell you exactly what to say.
I have the power,
Don't you see?
To make those pieces
Become a Masterpiece!
The scars you have,
The marks you see
Are thorns of beauty,
Be proud to be
Beloved Rose.
You are to me!

JOY

The Joy you bring into my life,
Your wonders always blow my mind.
You make me smile and I sigh…
You make me feel,
You make me see,
"I am your God.
"Abide by me."
That even in my silent cries,
When I pray, in silent mind,
If only I could see a sign,
And there it is, so high and bright!
I see a rainbow in the sky!
I can't deny,
I have no doubt
That this is you.
You do Respond,
I walk by faith because I see,
For what a Joy you bring to me!

My Keeper

You are my cover in the rain,
I know that you, too, see my pain,
You are my strength to stay in faith.
To know that you will always keep me safe…
No matter what my heart may feel,
That even when I am faced with fear,
When looking back, I now can see
The person that I used to be,
Your grace, Your love, has helped me see,
That You, my God!
Are that missing link…
The void that I have always felt was more that I could ever
bear.
I praise You, God, for now I see
That You have always been with me.
You hold my hand and walk me through,
Your promises you always keep.
Your guidance and your word I seek.
In joyful times,
In times of need,
You are my hope, O mighty King.
My keeper you will always be.

Hidden Treasure

You sent me a best friend to have
To hold each other hand in hand.
You send us to the world at once
To keep us in each other's arms.
To know that we were not alone,
Seeking for meaning of our pain,
Would be the compass
To guide our way,
To make us understand the pain.
That certain wounds were not in vain,
We prayed for You to break the chains!
With constant prayer
And with praise,
We followed clues that led the way.
It would take time to understand
The questions that would lead to truth.
To have no doubt that it was You!
The journeys of our lives you knew.
For you kept our brother safe.
To guard his heart from so much pain,
We will give glory to your name!
A hidden treasure broke a chain,
Our brother whom you know by name.

Forever by Your Side

Endless battles in my mind
Seem to keep me up at night.
Will this torture ever end?
I close my eyes,
Try to make sense.

It wasn't a coincidence…
God heard me pray for an escape!

He told me, "I will make a way,
It's not an easy path to take.
The battles for you I will win*!*
I'll be the one to give you strength.
Protector of your heart and mind.
No matter what you face in life,
I'll be forever by your side.
That even when you think you lost,
We will together come out strong.
No one will question who you are,
For I am yours
And you are mine!"

Butterfly Wings

You welcome me,
O mighty King.
I wait until the day we meet.
Father God, you meet my needs,
Your grace has brought me out of dark,
That even my own blood may mock.
For following your ways in life,
I praise you, God, you are my rock!

Your love for me will be enough.
Your Spirit in me is my strength,
That even if my own betray,
You tell me, that for them to pray.
You build me up and give me wings.
The hope to see what lies beneath,
Potential in myself I see.
The power of your Word, my King,
They are your gift, my butterfly wings.

Lamp to My Feet

In these moments, when I wonder
What the outcome will be,
Father God, where are you?
Why are you letting this be?
Feeling like I'm drowning
in all the uncertainty!
Sleepless nights
Threaten my peace.
I come back to reality,
It is you, that pulls me back,
Reminding me
It is not your will
But mine!
Don't you see?
There's no point in worrying,
For I am in control of everything!
You tell me, "Count your blessings,
What have I given thee?"
It is when I bow my head and say,
"Father God, forgive me.
It is you who fights my battles.
You will bring me victory!
I don't need to try to solve
Or make sense of anything!
For you are the light to follow,
To fulfill my destiny!"

Wonders

Feeling so frail, about to break,
The pain is unbearable,
It's hard not to shake, give me the courage
That I need in moments I feel I need to scream!

You tell me to show you those hidden places,
"The ones you think I haven't seen!
Weak attempt to hide your tears,
Daughter of mine, speak to me!"

"Although you think I do not see,
I am moving behind the scenes,
Come to me, tell me, where is your faith?
Don't allow fear to overtake, be strong,
Abide by me,
I will give you what you need."'

"Those moments when you cried yourself to sleep,
Let me remind you that I know everything,
Even the desires you hide so deep.
The ones you never dared to ask,
That even then it will be humanly impossible to grasp.
My wonders to you are gifts of love,
For I am the everlasting God!"

"Wonders uniquely made just for you!
You will have no doubt they come from me.
Wonders that will astonish others,
But for you, my daughter…
They will be so clear to see!"

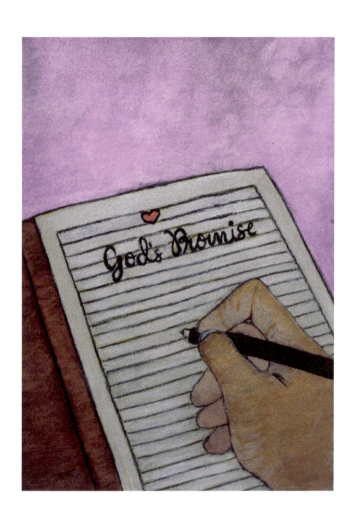

Promise of God

Every single step I took,
I prayed for you
To guide me through.
You show your power
Day by day
When answered prayers
Come my way!
You knew me
Way before I came,
That even in,
My name I see
Your perfect plan
For me to be.
It didn't matter what it took,
You knew exactly what to do!
You knew the hardships
I would face,
The routes I would decide to take,
Amazing God, You are alive,
You've set aside
The plan that would reroute my life.
For when your perfect time would come,
Nothing could ever block my way
To come to you, and with you stay.
It's like a special bond we have,
Just how I hear you, in my dreams.
You are my promise,
Yes, you are!
The meaning of your name, that is!

Special note from author: The meaning of Elisa, my name, is promise of God

Letter to My Love

The way you prayed,
The way you praised,
It really caught my heart
Off guard!!
I prayed for it
To go away,
But it got stronger
Day by day.
I don't want to get hurt again,
The fear of making a mistake.
My heart was hurt,
I was betrayed.
I pray for God to let me know,
To have no doubt
That it is you,
The one
That he kept hidden…
Just for me.
I've never met someone like you.
Your confidence,
Your poise so strong,
I prayed to God
To guard my heart
Until the day
I know your name.
I pray to God
To keep you safe.
This letter to my love,
I'll save.
Until the day we meet and dance,
I'll keep this letter at a glance!

Amor Real

Al buscar amor, en el mundo…
Grave Error yo cometí…
Pues el que decía Amarme,
Con su Tiranía, y Golpes,
Poco a Poco me perdí…

Derrotada y sin fuerzas,
Me dijiste,
"Ven A mi!"

En tus ojos reflejaste,
El dolor de verme así,

¡No me reprochaste Nada!
Me dijiste,
"Mírame"

Con dulzura me mostraste,
Todo lo que, vez en Mí,

Con tu Amor, Tú Me sanaste,
Cuando yo vine hacia a ti,

Me dijiste,
"Algún día, muy Cercano,
Yo ya tengo para ti,"

"Ese anhelo tan deseado,
Que te cuesta describir,"

"El que sigue mis caminos,
Y tu nombre ya le di."

Quizas

Desde el día que te vi
Sentí una conexión Algo que no tiene explicación.

Como un Imán, Cuando atrae,
Un pedazo de metal,

Trataba de no mirar
Pero, Era inevitable voltear

Y no sentir Lo que sentí
Quizás,
Nunca lo sabrás,
Lo que tu provocas, En mí,

Lo guardare En el fondo de mi ser,
Hasta el día que te vuelva a ver.

Quizás lo que yo siento, Es solo una ilusión,
Quizás, en esto quede
En Una simple emoción,

Yo no pienso delatarme,
Ya que tú debes de conquistarme.
Y Con eso me conformo,
Con el que quizás un día,
Tú te atreves, A buscarme.

Scattered Pieces

She bore a child she didn't want.
In her eyes, we ruined her life,
Constant longing for that love,
Sadly would not ever come.

Inflicted pain we didn't deserve
From all the Rage she had in Reserve!

Heal those pieces that are so torn!
It seems impossible for glue to hold!

Scattered pieces of my heart,
Felt so lost,
I had no hope,
Different ways I tried to cope,
Made me feel just so alone.

Gathered them into your hands,
Showing me your mighty plan!
"Don't you see just who I am?
Elohim,
The great I Am!
I will heal you,
Walk you through…
Scattered pieces
I'll make new!"

Follow Me

Like the breeze of the wind
Touched me
So tenderly,
Becoming one,
Loving me
Intentionally,
For God has sent you to me,
Pruning our flaws
Until the day we meet.

God said,
"Until your heart is mine,
I will lead you to your wife-to-be!
For a man after my heart,
He shall abide by me…
For a treasure
You'll both find…
True love and light
Just follow me…

El es

Es incredible describir
Lo que tu Jesus, haz hecho en mi
Cuando me me preguntan
Como es?

Todo dolor y toda traición,
Es como una herida abierta,
Que la vuelven a reabrir,
Con una Sonrisa, Yo les digo
Es que no soy yo,
Eterno Dios, El es!
Es mi fuerza de seguir!

Se sorprenden al saber, que mi fe…
Sigue firme
Sigue alli!

Y les digo,
"Es el rey de los cielos, El Principe de paz!"
"El que no me dejara Jamás!"
Toda Honra al El!
Rey de reyes como El,
No hay otro Mas!

Don't Look Back

Throughout my life, you helped me fight
Some battles big, Some battles small…
But you've been with me all along!

You lead my way
From dark to light

Wiping my tears,
Changing my fears…

You knew the pain
The SHAME!
The BLAME!

Your voice so tender, yet so strong
Guiding me ALL this time…

Telling me,
"Forget the past, and don't look back
"For all the joy I bring,
Will last!"

The Dream

You walked with me
Side by side
Keeping me strong in the fight!

You engraved into my heart!
For it is now, I understand
Why I am, who I am!
I am here to fulfill your plan!

Use my father
For I am glad!
I leave my every fear in your hands!
Obeying your every command!
Completely surrendering my life!
Will bring me into the light!

For now, I see that as I walked
I fought my flesh
I let it die!
Your Spirit led me
To the dream
The one
You keep within my reach
To keep you in my heart to teach!
Search my thoughts
Oh, mighty King!
For when it's time,
To speak your Word!
Your perfect plan
Will change the world!

My Heart Is Yours

Train my heart to what is yours,
For I am the one you chose,
Guard my heart, and keep it close…

Fill me with your Spirit, and help me discern…
What it is that I am feeling…and what I've already been told.

For you always keep your promise… And I never walk alone!

You have RESCUED me from darkness,
Oh, the darkness you've made lit!

May I always be reminded, to align (my heart) it with your word!

For You rule the world!
Move mountains!
As you sit upon your THRONE!
For I pray to always honor and obey your every word.

Marvelous Names

I exalt your Name to ALL who hear!
For you, My God, keep my heart so near!
I believe my father lives!
For you, Jireh
Supply ALL my needs!

For you, My King,
Took all the shame!
For you are, Love!
Love me like no other, call me yours
Call me by Name

For you, My Father
Never change!
For You are,
Alpha and Omega!
Always the same,

For you are,
The Way Maker!
Promise Keeper!
All I need to do is trust and wait!

Father God I see,
You're GREAT!
I will not forget to PROCLAIM!

Your Mighty and Many Marvelous Names!

Inside Out

I am transformed inside out!
I will declare, Jesus's Name!
I will no longer
Be afraid!
I'll let you, Father,
Mold my shape…
You will heal my heart in a way,

Leading others where You Reign!
We will worship and proclaim!
Abba, Father, Your mighty name!

I will stand, and I will shout!
I am transformed inside out!

Lead my way to hear your voice,
Use your power to mute the Noise!

I am here, and I am Yours,
Lead me father, Open Doors!

Help my heart and mind to be,
Where the focus needs to be,
That your WILL,
Shall be complete.

You Changed Me

All my life I've been afraid,
To speak my mind!
To have a say!

Piece by piece, You took away…
The fear, the thoughts
That made me stay…
Submerged in darkness and in pain…

You told me,
"I will peel away,
The layers of doubt,
That piled every day!…"

The fears of the "HOW?"
I will swipe away!

For I give you strength,
That no one can take!

The courage to stand,
To let the words flow,
To let the world know!
To give others freedom,
Just as I freed you,
The moment I saved you!

BE STILL

In those moments when it rains,
It won't always be the same,

Trust in me, and I'll be,
Always with you, when you seek.

I'll protect you,
Be your Guide!
Not to worry call my name!
Promise Keeper,
Great I am!

All your chaos, I will change!

Not to worry,
Don't you see?
Things aren't always what they seem!
Seek my presence, and you'll see

That my promise I will keep!

My All

I will love you with my all!
Abba Father,
You're My Rock!

From beginning till the end!
You will guide me, give me strength!
All the storms,
You will withstand!

I will come to you and pray…
To not ever go astray!

You have shown me,
You're the Light!
All my battles you will fight!

I will love you with my All!
You won't ever let me fall!

Sacred Love

Seeking acceptance and validation,
I looked for love in the wrong places.

Your Love for me is sacred,
One of a kind!
How could I have been so blind!

You took my shattered heart,
You promised me to put it back.

Piece by piece,
You placed them back.

You bring me peace,
Making me feel complete!

Your love for me will never die.

I will forever call you mine,
For until the end of time!

Father God!
You are my Knight!
Your Love is pure!

No other love can withstand time.

Tu Essencia

No fue al instante
Que yo te vi!
Si no poco a poco…

Sin que te dieras cuenta,
Despertastes
Algo muy fuerte,
Dentro de mi!

Por temor a este sentimiento…
Trate de alejarte de mi…

Con mi comportamiento…
Te confundi…

Pensaste que mi indiferencia,
Fue por ti,
Mas sin embargo…
Fue en ese momento…
Que yo entendí…

Poco a poco,
Algo muy especial
Crecia dentro de mi,
Pues, de Tu Essencia…

Sin darme cuenta…
Me enamore de ti…

About the Author

A bilingual, Elisa Dominguez is a divorcee and a mother of three. She began writing by journaling her prayers throughout this difficult time, discovering her passion for writing. She writes faith-based poetry, mostly about her conversations with God, and also a few that are romantic and love-inspired. She credits Jesus Christ for her faith and gift.

Elisa is from Chicago, and she hopes to one day write romance books, travel, and share her testimony to others who might be struggling through difficult times. She wants to raise awareness regarding domestic violence, mental health, emotional and physical abuse.

You may contact the author through

elisa.domingz@gmail.com
tiktok.com/@elisa.domingz
https://instagram.com/elisa.domingz?igshid=iayoeu1am0at

CPSIA information can be obtained
at www.ICGtesting.com
Printed in the USA
BVHW090336221221
624588BV00010B/852